D1413713

BIOGRAPHY FROM
ANCIENT CIVILIZATIONS
LEGENDS, FOLKLORE, AND STORIES OF ANCIENT WORLDS

*The Life and Times of*

# CLEOPATRA

## Mitchell Lane
### PUBLISHERS

P.O. Box 196
Hockessin, Delaware 19707

# BIOGRAPHY FROM ANCIENT CIVILIZATIONS
## LEGENDS, FOLKLORE, AND STORIES OF ANCIENT WORLDS

## Titles in the Series

*The Life and Times of:*

BIOGRAPHY FROM
ANCIENT CIVILIZATIONS
LEGENDS, FOLKLORE, AND STORIES OF ANCIENT WORLDS

*The Life and Times of*

# CLEOPATRA

*Michelle Medlock Adams*

Printing          1          2          3          4          5          6          7          8

Library of Congress Cataloging-in-Publication Data

Adams, Michelle Medlock.
　　The life and times of Cleopatra / by Michelle Medlock Adams.
　　　　p. cm. — (Biography from ancient civilizations)
　　Includes bibliographical references and index.
　　ISBN 1-58415-335-0 (library bound)
　　1. Cleopatra, Queen of Egypt, d. 30 B.C.—Juvenile literature. 2. Egypt—History—332-30 B.C.—Juvenile literature. 3. Queens—Egypt—Biography—Juvenile literature. I. Title. II. Series.
　　932'.021—dc22

2004024415

ABOUT THE AUTHOR: Earning first-place awards from the Associated Press, the Hoosier State Press Association, and the Society of Professional Journalists, Michelle Medlock Adams has published more than 3,000 articles in newspapers and magazines around the country. She has also authored 15 books, including her award-winning picture book, "Conversations On the Ark." She graduated from Indiana University with a journalism degree in 1991, and has been writing professionally ever since. She and her husband, Jeff, and their two daughters, Abby and Allyson, make their home in Texas with their three miniature dachshunds.

PHOTO CREDITS: Cover, p. 2, p. 6, p. 20, p. 34: Jamie Kondrchek; p. 8, 11, 12, 15, 30, 40: Corbis; p. 22, 36: Getty Images

PUBLISHER'S NOTE: This story is based on the author's extensive research, which she believes to be accurate. Documentation of such research is contained on page 46.

The internet sites referenced herein were active as of the publication date. Due to the fleeting nature of some web sites, we cannot guarantee they will all be active when you are reading this book.

CHAPTER

# ONE

# HISTORY'S GREATEST QUEEN

Cleopatra VII, queen of Egypt from 51 to 30 B.C., is truly one of the most mysterious and memorable women in history. If she were alive today, her name and her picture would be plastered across the pages of tabloids and celebrity magazines on a regular basis. She was a diva, a goddess, a powerful woman, a seductress and Egypt's last pharaoh. Not only was she wealthy beyond belief, but she also had quite a wild life, according to historical accounts.

She was an aggressive woman. She had romances with two of ancient history's most powerful men—first with Julius Caesar, and after Caesar's death, with Mark Antony. Legend says that Cleopatra dressed as Aphrodite, the Greek goddess of love, when she traveled to meet Antony and win his heart. It worked! Antony was smitten by her charms.

He wasn't the only one. She seemed to cast a sort of hypnotic spell over all of the men in her life.

"Cleopatra is a person to be wondered at..." wrote a French poet and novelist named Theophile Gautier, "whom dreamers find always at the end of their dreams."[1]

Cicero, a famous Roman who lived during the first century B.C., said, "Her character, which pervaded her actions in an inexplicable

*Posing as Isis, Cleopatra is captured in this stone wall plaque. This seems fitting, since Cleopatra was often compared to such goddesses and considered to be superhuman by some of her greatest fans.*

way when meeting people, was utterly spellbinding. The sound of her voice was sweet when she talked."[2]

However, she wasn't just a sweet talker. She had everything— power, wealth, charm, beauty and wisdom. She knew how to get what she wanted. Many people loved her; other people loved to hate her. Even today, Cleopatra continues to intrigue historians and enthusiasts of ancient Egypt. One of the main reasons why she is so intriguing is that no one is certain what is myth and what is truth concerning Cleopatra. Many things documented about her conflict with one another. When she was in power, the press didn't strive for unbiased reporting. Romans recorded most of what was documented about Cleopatra, but the Romans tended to greatly dislike her. Most loyal Romans loathed her because she wasn't Roman; she was the queen of Egypt. They believed that she corrupted Caesar and Mark Antony. For that reason, fact and fiction become entangled when it comes to many of the details of Cleopatra's colorful days on earth. But one thing is certain: she lived an exciting, eventful life.

When Cleopatra became the queen of Egypt at the age of eighteen, she wasn't a typical teenager. She was wise beyond her years. She didn't rule the country all by herself. In keeping with Egyptian custom, she shared the crown with her brothers Ptolemy XIII (51-47 BC) and Ptolemy XIV (47-44 BC).

She quickly learned that her wisdom and womanly wiles would be needed to survive and thrive. One of the most famous stories about Cleopatra occurred a few years after she first took the throne. She found herself caught in the middle of a power struggle between Julius Caesar and Pompey the Great, another important Roman leader. By that time, conflicts with her brother Ptolemy XIII had forced her to flee from Alexandria, the capital of Egypt.

When Caesar defeated Pompey, he considered Egypt to be Roman property. He came to Alexandria and summoned Cleopatra and Ptolemy XIII to a meeting at the royal palace. He wanted to resolve their conflict.

With good reason, Cleopatra feared that her enemies might kill her if she publicly set foot in Alexandria. So she slipped into the city during the hours of darkness with a single servant. She had the servant wrap her inside a large rug. Then he carried the rug into the palace and laid it down in front of Caesar. At that point, she unwrapped herself and presented herself to the most powerful man in Rome. It's been said that Caesar fell in love with Cleopatra that very night. He took her side in the dispute with her brother, ordering that the two of them should marry (according to the custom of their family) and rule together. This was what their father's will had called for. Her sneaky rug trick and womanly charms had served her well.

She used that same charm and craftiness throughout her rule, making her mysteriously endearing. She may have been the Marilyn Monroe of ancient times. In a strange twist of fate, both of these famous beauties ended their lives through suicide.

As one might expect of an ancient diva, Cleopatra has been the subject of many plays, poems, books, and articles through the centuries. More than two dozen movies have been made about her. Perhaps the most famous was made in 1963 and starred Elizabeth Taylor as Cleopatra. Even today, Cleopatra continues to dazzle the world. Her legend lives on, and as legends often do, it grows a bit with each year.

# Cleopatra on the Silver Screen

**FYI**
For Your Info

The name "Cleopatra" has become synonymous with extravagance and elegance. Those qualities were evident when the Queen came to the silver screen back in 1963 in *Cleopatra*. The Twentieth Century Fox film cost $44 million to make, which would be nearly $300 million by today's standards.

Why did it cost so much to make? There were several reasons. The first was actress Elizabeth Taylor's base salary of one million dollars. She was the very first actor to reach that level of income for a film. If that weren't enough, her overtime pay brought her check to about $7,000,000 by the time the film was finished. Also, the producers were forced to relocate shooting from London to Italy because of rain delays and Elizabeth Taylor's life-threatening bout with pneumonia. All of the expensive sets in London had to be scrapped and new ones were built. New actors had to be hired and many scenes had to be re-shot.

Still another problem was that the actors who had originally been cast to play the major male roles of Julius Caesar and Mark Antony had to leave their roles. The delayed filming of *Cleopatra* overlapped their other film commitments. Rex Harrison (Julius Caesar) and Richard Burton (Mark Antony) were signed to replace them. The addition of Burton proved a very satisfactory choice for Liz Taylor. Like the original Queen Cleopatra and Mark Antony, she and Burton had an extremely well-publicized romance of their own off-screen. Their affair fueled the promotion of the movie, making it a must-see for many moviegoers.

Though it was very expensive to produce, breaking industry records and almost breaking the bank, the movie finally did prove its worth, both financially and artistically. It was one of the highest grossing films of the 1960s and was nominated for eight Academy Awards, winning four: special effects, costume design, cinematography and art direction.

*Actress Elizabeth Taylor is seen here in full costume and makeup from a scene in "Cleopatra" released in 1963.*

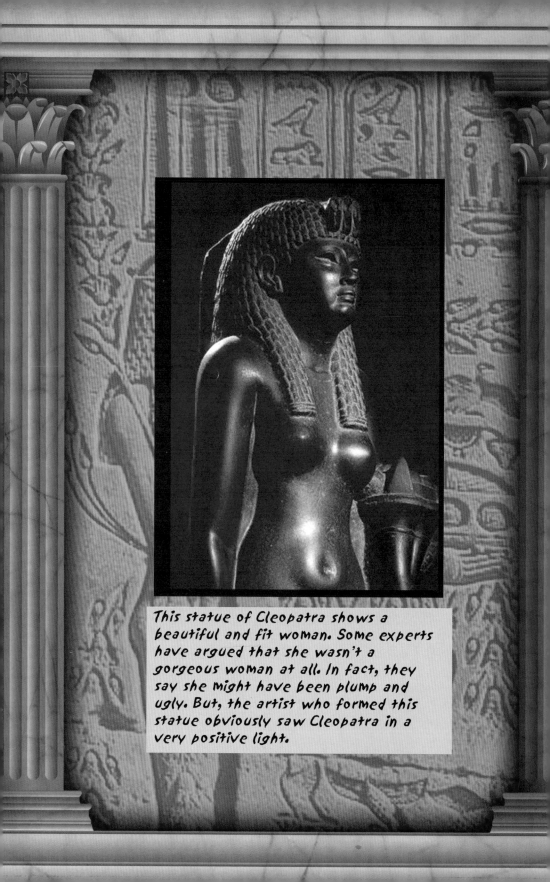

This statue of Cleopatra shows a beautiful and fit woman. Some experts have argued that she wasn't a gorgeous woman at all. In fact, they say she might have been plump and ugly. But, the artist who formed this statue obviously saw Cleopatra in a very positive light.

## CHAPTER TWO

# THE TEEN QUEEN

Cleopatra was born in 69 BC in Alexandria. She came from a long line of rulers. Her father, Ptolemy XII (more familiarly known as "The Flute-Player" for his love of music), was Egypt's pharaoh. Her mother was probably Cleopatra V, but historians aren't entirely sure. Cleopatra had two older sisters, Cleopatra VI and Berenice; two younger brothers, Ptolemy XIII and Ptolemy XIV, who were born in 61 and 59 BC; and a younger sister, Arsinoe. While all of her siblings would be a large part of Egypt's history, Cleopatra is by far the most memorable member of her family.

Though Cleopatra's ancestors had ruled Egypt for many years, they were not Egyptian. They originally came from Macedonia. The family was descended from Ptolemy I, a general of Alexander the Great. Ptolemy I became the king of Egypt after Alexander's death in 323 BC when his empire was divided among the three most powerful Macedonian generals. Ptolemy took Egypt, Antigonus took Macedonia and most of Asia Minor (modern-day Turkey), while Seleucis ruled Syria and the lands to the east.

Cleopatra's father was not a great ruler. Some accounts say he was a drunkard and a weak man. His people did not respect him.

At this time, Rome wanted control over Egypt. The Roman Republic was swallowing up a great deal of land. As a result, it needed

Egypt's grain to help feed the many mouths in its new conquests. Rome was hoping to gain rule over Egypt in the near future.

One of the most important Roman leaders was Pompey the Great. In 60 BC, he formed an alliance, often referred to as the First Triumvirate, with his fellow Romans Crassus and Julius Caesar. The triumvirate considered taking Egypt by force. Ptolemy XII was aware of their power, especially the formidable Roman soldiers that they commanded.

The following year, Ptolemy offered the triumvirs a bribe of 6,000 talents so that he could be officially considered a friend of the Roman people. Talents were units of money used in ancient Greece, Rome and the Middle East. The bribe was fine with the triumvirs. They believed that they could convince Ptolemy to do whatever they needed. Six thousand talents was a lot of money back then. In fact, some experts say it was equal to the profits from one year's worth of trading in Egypt.

There was only one problem: Ptolemy didn't actually have the money to give the triumvirate. He had to borrow it from a Roman banker named Gaius Rabirius Postumus. He didn't want anyone in Egypt to know about his loan, but the secret was revealed soon after.

In 57 BC, the Romans took over Cyprus, which had been part of the Ptolemies' empire for more than 200 years. At the time of the takeover, the island was ruled by the brother of Ptolemy XII, who ended his life when he lost his throne. The loss of the island plus the additional taxes that Ptolemy XII had imposed in order to pay off the loan made the king even more unpopular in Egypt. He was forced to flee from Egypt and go to Rome. It's believed that he took Cleopatra with him.

With Ptolemy in Rome, the new co-rulers of Egypt were his daughters Cleopatra VI and Berenice. Ptolemy XII asked his friends in Rome to assist him in regaining his throne. Rabirius, the banker,

*This statue of Pompey the Great captures the worry of a man with much on his mind. In real life, that was very true. Pompey was a Roman general and statesman who was part of the very first Triumvirate with Julius Caesar and Crassus.*

pressured Pompey and Caesar to help Ptolemy return so that he could resume the repayment of his loan. Meanwhile, Ptolemy's daughters made a case against their father, accusing him of many improper actions. They even sent witnesses to these improprieties to Rome to testify on their behalf, but the witnesses were killed once they entered Italy. It seems that Ptolemy was able to gain favor with the Romans.

Ptolemy left Rome and traveled eastward. He made a deal with Aulus Gabinius, the governor of the Roman province of Syria. Gabinius agreed to help Ptolemy regain his throne for a fee of 10,000 talents. As Ptolemy thought about this proposition, one of Gabinius's young officers named Mark Antony convinced him to take the deal. Though Ptolemy didn't know if he would ever be able to repay his debt, he figured he would continue receiving Rome's support if he took the money. The Roman leaders would want him to stay in power so that he could pay off his debt.

Back in Alexandria, Cleopatra VI disappeared from the throne. No one knows what happened to her. As a result, Berenice was left alone and in need of a co-ruler. She first married a young man who was a descendent of Seleucis, but she ended up disliking him so much that she had him strangled to death. Next, she arranged a marriage with Archelaus, a prince from an area just south of the Black Sea. Archelaus didn't last long. He was killed when Gabinius led his forces into Egypt on Ptolemy's behalf. Historians believe that this may have been when Mark Antony and Cleopatra first met. She was only about 14 at the time. Their love affair wouldn't begin for well over a decade.

Ptolemy XII regained his throne in 55 BC. One of his first acts was to order the execution of his daughter Berenice. But Ptolemy was hardly his own man. Gabinius and Rabirius, who were responsible for his restoration, stayed on in important positions so they could milk Egypt for all it was worth. Eventually, the two greedy men were run out of Alexandria, although Julius Caesar assured Rabirius that he would get his money back for him.

Ptolemy ruled for four years after regaining the throne. His position was so shaky that Gabinius had to leave soldiers behind to support him. When Ptolemy died in 51 BC, his will named eighteen-year-old Cleopatra and ten-year-old Ptolemy XIII as his heirs. In view of her family's murderous history, historian Andrew Meadows notes that "Cleopatra did not so much ascend a throne as descend into a snake-pit."[1]

As co-ruler, Cleopatra was young, but she had much to offer her kingdom. She even spoke nine languages. In fact, she was the first Ptolemaic pharaoh who could actually speak Egyptian.

Even though she had to marry Ptolemy XIII, it was a marriage of convenience as was traditional for the pharaohs. As the male, he had power over her; however, he was too young to rule so she wanted to rule alone while he grew up. She even issued coins that showed only her likeness. Ruling alone seemed the right thing to do, but Ptolemy XIII's advisors didn't like it. They disagreed with her on many issues, but they really hated her desire to maintain Rome's support. Led by a eunuch named Pothinus, they plotted against Cleopatra and finally ran her out of Egypt in 48 BC.

There were other problems in Egypt at that time. It's been recorded that there were crop failures in 50 and 49 BC. These caused the Egyptian people to become quite restless, as well.

Cleopatra wasn't easily shaken. Ptolemy's advisors didn't count on the fact that she had supporters beyond Alexandria. Unlike most of her predecessors, she had a way with people. As the historian Plutarch commented, "To know her was to be touched with an irresistible charm. Her form, coupled with the persuasiveness of her conversation, and her delightful style of behavior—all these produced a blend of magic. Her delightful manner of speaking was such as to win the heart. Her voice was like a lyre."[2]

These outside supporters were willing to help her regain her crown, so she put together an army and headed for Egypt's border. Meanwhile, Julius Caesar had seized the upper hand for control of the Roman Republic. Crassus had been killed in 53 BC during a disastrous battle in Parthia, an empire located in modern-day Iraq and Iran. Four years later, Caesar and Pompey clashed in a bloody civil war in Italy. Pompey fled to Greece, where he lost the battle of Pharsalus in 48 BC. He sailed to Alexandria to seek protection from Ptolemy, with Caesar right on his heels. Ptolemy's advisors decided to side with Caesar instead and stabbed Pompey to death. They beheaded Pompey and sent his head to Caesar as a gift. Caesar was very disturbed by Pompey's brutal death, so he marched into Alexandria and took control of the palace. His first act of business was to try to get Cleopatra and her brother together to settle their power struggle.

It was at this crucial moment that Cleopatra wrapped herself up in a rug and snuck inside the palace. She presented herself to Caesar. Historians say that she and Caesar became involved with each other that very night. He was instantly struck by her charm and beauty.

When Ptolemy saw Caesar and Cleopatra together, he became enraged. He told everyone that he had been betrayed. Caesar wouldn't allow Ptolemy to leave the palace. Cleopatra's sister Arsinoe managed to escape and proclaimed herself co-ruler with Ptolemy. Their supporters attacked the palace. Caesar decided it would be best to release Ptolemy to appease the attackers, but the war continued for another six months. It ended when Caesar's troops defeated the

Egyptians. Ptolemy drowned in the Nile while trying to escape. Alexandria returned to Caesar's control, and he captured Arsinoe in order to return the throne to Cleopatra. As tradition demanded, Cleopatra married her other brother Ptolemy XIV, who was only 11 or 12 years old.

Then she set off on a "honeymoon cruise" on the Nile River; however, it wasn't with her new husband. It was with Julius Caesar.

# Caesar—More Than A Salad!

Gaius Julius Caesar was born on July 13, 100 BC and was killed on the Ides of March (March 15), 44 BC. But, during his life, he lived every day to its fullest.

By age 39, Julius Caesar had accomplished more than most men will accomplish in an entire lifetime. At one time, he was adored by practically everyone in Rome. He was made imperator by his troops, consul and pontifex maximus (high priest)—an esteemed honor usually reserved for the end of a man's career.

It would seem there was nothing left for him to accomplish in the remaining 17 years of his life, yet those years were maybe more notable than his first 39. He became part of the first Triumvirate, had many military victories in Gaul, revamped the government, and became Cleopatra's lover and father to her son, Caesarian, to name a few accomplishments.

Some historians have said that Caesar's biggest mistake may have been becoming too powerful, thus becoming too much of a threat for his one-time supporters. He was brutally murdered by those he trusted. Historian and writer Plutarch recorded the events this way:

"So it began, and those who were not in the conspiracy were so horrorstruck and amazed at what was being done that they were afraid to run away and afraid to come to Caesar's help; they were too afraid even to utter a word. But those who had come prepared for the murder all bared their daggers and hemmed Caesar in on every side. Whichever way he turned he met the blows of daggers and saw the cold steel aimed at his face and at his eyes. So he was driven this way and that, and like a wild beast in the toils, had to suffer from the hands of each of them; for it had been agreed that they must all take part in this sacrifice and all flesh themselves with his blood...Some say that Caesar fought back against all the rest, darting this way and that to avoid the blows and crying out for help, but when he saw that Brutus had drawn his dagger, he covered his head with his toga and sank down to the ground." (Plutarch, Life, 66.) [3]

Caesar's death left a big hole in Rome. Some say he was the very heart and soul of Rome. One thing is for sure—his life and death made a huge impact on history. A few historians have declared that Caesar was the greatest man of all time. All in all, he was a passionate leader who lived and died in a larger-than-life way.

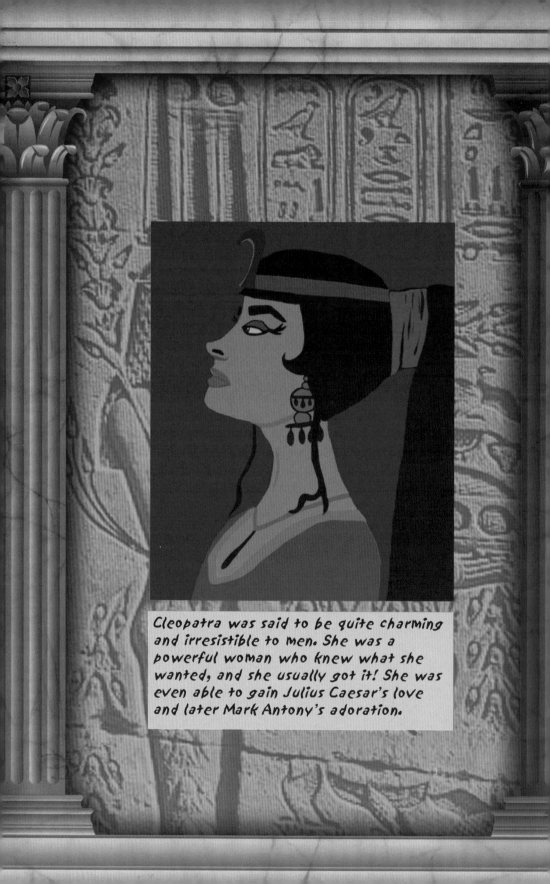

Cleopatra was said to be quite charming and irresistible to men. She was a powerful woman who knew what she wanted, and she usually got it! She was even able to gain Julius Caesar's love and later Mark Antony's adoration.

## CHAPTER
# THREE

# LOVE AND WAR

As Julius Caesar embarked on his cruise with Cleopatra, he was in his early 50s—quite a bit older than Cleopatra. However, he was a powerful, attractive man with quite a reputation. According to historian Arthur Weigall, "He was an extremely active soldier, a clever, graceful swordsman, a powerful swimmer, and an excellent athlete. In battle he had proved himself brave, gallant and cool-headed; and in his earlier years he had been regarded as a dashing young officer…Already at the age of twenty-one he had won the Civic Crown, the Victoria Cross of that period, for saving a soldier's life at the storming of Mytilene"[1]

The age difference didn't seem to bother Caesar or Cleopatra, and their love was sealed on the cruise, which lasted for at least two months. They were very smitten with one another, particularly because Cleopatra was pregnant. The child was almost certainly Caesar's.

According to the Alexandrian Greek Athenaeus, their royal barge was "about three hundred feet long, forty-five feet on the beam, and rising about sixty feet above water. It was not so much a ship as a floating palace. It was propelled by several banks of oars, and

*Julius Caesar, easily the most powerful man in the world at that time, was quite a bit older than Cleopatra, yet they fell in love anyway. He was said to be quite attractive for a man in his 50s.*

contained banqueting rooms, colonnades and courtyards, shrines and garden areas."[2] It would have rivaled the most luxurious cruise ships of today.

After the long boat ride, Caesar returned to Rome. During his conquests and battles, Cleopatra remained in his mind. He sent for her a year later. By then she had given birth to a son. Formally, the boy was named Ptolemy XV Caesar. Cleopatra called him "Caesarion," which meant "Little Caesar." Not everyone was happy about Cleopatra's baby boy. Cornelius Oppius, a friend of Caesar's, wrote a pamphlet designed to "prove" that Caesarion was not Caesar's son. Despite the pamphlet, however, virtually everyone assumed that the boy was Caesar's. Contemporary descriptions of Caesarion indicate that he did look a lot like Caesar.

Cleopatra arrived in Rome in the fall of 46 BC. She brought along Caesarion and her younger brother/husband Ptolemy XIV. It was a time of celebration in Rome, and Caesar was making the most of it. In September, he celebrated his recent war victories by parading through the streets with his prisoners—including Cleopatra's sister Arsinoe. Normally prisoners were executed after these public humiliations. Caesar spared Arsinoe's life and sent her into exile.

Cleopatra enjoyed her time in Rome so much that she decided to stay. She lived in Caesar's villa near Rome for almost two years. During that time, Caesar gave her many gifts and titles. He catered to her every whim. In fact, he even had a statue of her put in the temple of Venus Genetrix—a very high honor.

While Caesar lavished Cleopatra with gifts, his fellow Romans hurled insults at her and Caesar. Many of them felt he was simply having what we might today call "a mid-life crisis" and should return to his wife, Calpurnia. Rumors began circulating throughout Rome. People whispered that Caesar was planning to pass a law that would allow him to marry Cleopatra and make Caesarion his heir.

The marriage of Caesar and Cleopatra would have united the East and West, and Cleopatra would have become Caesar's queen-empress. Everything was turning out even better than she had imagined. Still, the Roman citizens were not thrilled with her, and they were becoming increasingly displeased with Caesar's affection for her.

They were also concerned about rumors that he intended to become king of Rome. He had already been appointed consul for five years and dictator indefinitely. People were calling him a god—beyond human limitations. He was without a doubt the most powerful man in the world.

During one of the celebrations, Mark Antony hailed Caesar as king and attempted to place a crown on his head. At this dramatic moment, several of Caesar's supporters yelled, "Accept! Accept!" He turned them down. He had no intention of accepting the crown that very day. He was simply "testing the waters" to see how the Roman people would react. Moments later, Antony tried again to crown Caesar but the crowd showed their disapproval. Rome had once been ruled by kings, but they had been overthrown several centuries before. So the crowd cheered when Caesar again rejected the crown. Caesar must have been quite disappointed in the crowd's reaction.

While many of the Roman people were convinced by Caesar's display in refusing the crown, others were not. Some believed that he was too ambitious. They were afraid that he still wanted to become king. Caesar's death was already being planned.

On March 15, 44 BC, the plan was carried out. A crowd of Caesar's enemies surrounded him at a Senate meeting. More than twenty of them pulled out their knives and stabbed him to death. Knowing that she, too, was in danger, Cleopatra took her son, her brother Ptolemy XIV, and their servants back to Egypt. Her dream of ruling over Egypt with Caesar died when Caesar was killed.

## The Future of Egypt

With Caesar's death, the Roman world was thrust into chaos. Romans mourned their former leader and were looking for a new one to restore order.

Mark Antony knew the mood of the Roman people—who were devastated by Caesar's death—and used that knowledge to his advantage when making the funeral speech for Caesar a few days after the murder. The speech, so beautifully embellished by Shakespeare, has become quite famous throughout the ages. It was a major blow to those who had arranged for Caesar's death. In this one powerful speech, Antony fondly remembered one of the greatest Roman rulers of all time and destroyed the influence of the conspirators. They were forced to flee for their lives.

Caesar's will named his eighteen-year-old grand-nephew Octavian as his heir. There was no mention of Caesarion at all. This must have surprised Cleopatra and deeply troubled her. She wasn't the only one who was troubled. So was Antony. He had risked his life on Caesar's behalf. He probably resented Octavian, believing that he himself should have been Caesar's heir.

At first, it didn't seem to matter. Antony was the most powerful man in Rome. But as with Caesar, some Romans feared his power. They thought they could take advantage of Octavian. Antony's enemies would use Octavian's connection with Caesar to get rid of Antony. Then they would get rid of Octavian. But that was a mistake. Octavian took advantage of the support that Antony's enemies offered. Soon he became as powerful as Antony. Together with a man named Lepidus, Antony and Octavian formed the Second Triumvirate in 43 BC.

To solidify their position in Rome, the triumvirs executed hundreds of potential opponents. The "hit list" included some men who had helped Octavian. These men had angered Antony, who wanted them dead. Octavian agreed, quickly proving that he would be ruthless in advancing his own interests.

The next step for the triumvirs was to hunt down and eliminate Julius Caesar's assassins. If they were successful, they would achieve supreme power.

*Julius Caesar*

Cleopatra was cunning and would do what was necessary to get what she wanted. She probably planned the murder of her brother, Ptolemy XIV.

## CHAPTER
# FOUR

# 'TIL DEATH DO US PART

Once Cleopatra was safely back in Egypt, she knew what she had to do—Ptolemy XIV needed to be killed. She probably orchestrated his death. By doing so, she was able to thrust Caesarion into the position of co-ruler of Egypt. It's doubtful that Caesarion realized what was happening, for he was only about three years old at the time.

With the death of Julius Caesar, Cleopatra had only one thing on her mind—ensuring that she and her son would continue to rule Egypt. She wanted to see how the power struggle in Rome would play out. Then she planned to align herself with whomever could help her retain her position.

Not long after she had returned to Egypt, Cleopatra was approached by Cassius, one of Caesar's assassins. He was seeking support for his cause in Syria, where he was in conflict with Dolabella, a former general of Caesar's. Dolabella also wanted Cleopatra's help. This presented a dilemma for Cleopatra because she didn't know which man to side with. Eventually, she sent military support to Dolabella. But Cassius defeated Dolabella, who committed suicide. The troops that Cleopatra sent went over to Cassius. Ironically, Cleopatra ended up helping the killers of her former love, Caesar.

Support for Cassius grew in Alexandria, and that worried Cleopatra. She was afraid if she didn't help him, the people in

Alexandria might turn on her and demand that her sister, Arsinoe, be brought out of exile to replace her on the throne.

As things turned out, her worries were in vain. Cassius and Brutus, the other primary conspirators against Caesar, soon took their war farther north, away from Egypt. That gave Cleopatra the chance to side with Octavian and Antony.

At the Battle of Philippi in northern Greece in 42 BC, the forces of Antony and Octavian defeated troops led by Brutus and Cassius, who committed suicide. Cleopatra had to be pleased with that news. It was confirmation that she had backed the right men. It seemed that her joint rule with Caesarion was sealed because Rome recognized their positions as rulers over Egypt. She had survived yet another crisis.

Cleopatra learned that Octavian was to be in control of the western half of the Roman territories, while Antony would oversee the eastern half. Lepidus, the least important of the triumvirs, was given North Africa. This division pleased Antony because he wanted to finish what Julius Caesar had started—laying claim to lands beyond the eastern border of the empire. That meant war with Parthia, an empire that had been nothing but trouble to Rome in recent years. One of his primary objectives in this war was to avenge the defeat and death of Crassus, Caesar's colleague in the original triumvirate, in 53 BC. He had another reason. Despite their alliance in the Second Triumvirate, Antony and Octavian deeply distrusted each other. The wealth and prestige that Antony would acquire with a victory over the Parthians could enable him to become more powerful than Octavian.

Antony realized that Cleopatra could provide much-needed financial help for this war. So he sent one of his officers with a request for her to meet him at the city of Tarsus (on the southern coast of modern-day Turkey) in the summer of 41 BC. Cleopatra had studied Antony, and she began planning the meeting. She didn't come when he first beckoned for her. Instead, she made him wait. Then she put on quite a show for him. She made her appearance in an elaborately decorated barge with a gold-plated stern, silver oars, purple sails, and an entire staff of slaves to fan her. The barge was covered with rose petals so that Antony and the other Romans could smell the fragrance before they even saw the vessel. She dressed herself in rich silks to resemble Aphrodite, the Greek goddess of love, and made her grand entrance.

The Queen's arrival made quite a splash. She wanted to impress Antony, and her strategy worked to perfection. The fact that a royal goddess would show interest in him flattered his male ego. Antony didn't care that he was already married, to a woman named Fulvia. He quickly fell in love with Cleopatra. By the time of their meeting, it was too late in the year to continue his military campaign. He chose to spend the winter in Alexandria with Cleopatra. Part of the attraction between the two of them was political. Cleopatra could supply Antony with money. In turn, he could protect her position on the throne of Egypt.

Another part of the attraction appears to have been genuine affection. By all reports Antony was a handsome man. In his early 40s, he was in the prime of life and enjoyed having a good time. He in turn was drawn to Cleopatra. Some sources say that she was able to get anything from Antony that she wanted. This included the assassination of her sister, Arsinoe. Cleopatra had now outlived all her siblings.

The Greek biographer Plutarch wrote about Cleopatra and Antony, "Plato [a famous Greek philosopher] admits four sorts of flattery, but she had a thousand. Were Antony serious or disposed to mirth, she had at any moment some new delight or charm to meet his wishes; at every turn she was upon him, and let him escape her neither by day nor by night. She played at dice with him, drank with him, hunted with him; and when he exercised in arms, she was there to see. At night she would go rambling with him to disturb and torment people at their doors and windows, dressed like a servant-woman, for Antony also went in servant's disguise…However, the Alexandrians in general liked it all well enough, and joined good-humouredly and kindly in his frolic and play."[1]

*Richard Burton and Elizabeth Taylor masterfully portrayed Antony and Cleopatra in the 1963 blockbuster film, "Cleopatra." Just like the script, Burton and Taylor fell madly in love, making their onscreen romance even better!*

When spring came, Antony had to leave. During his absence from Rome, his wife Fulvia had helped to organize a revolt against Octavian. It failed, and Fulvia fled to Greece. She became ill and died there. Antony knew that it was important to patch things up with Octavian. He wasn't ready for an open split. So he returned to Rome and married Octavian's sister, Octavia. She was quite pretty and recently widowed, as well. She had three children from her previous marriage and quickly bore Antony a daughter.

Meanwhile, Cleopatra had delivered twins—a boy and a girl, fathered by Antony. She named them Alexander Helios (sun) and Cleopatra Selene (moon).

It's likely that the news of Antony's marriage distressed Cleopatra. She had no way of knowing if he would ever return to her. But if she was worried, she couldn't allow it to show. By most accounts, she spent the next three years working hard to rule Egypt in a fair and just fashion. Most of her predecessors had ruled primarily for their own benefit without much concern for the welfare of the Egyptians. By contrast, Cleopatra appears to have earned the loyalty and admiration of the people. She was especially concerned with making sure that everyone had enough to eat. It also helped that with her brothers and sisters all dead, there was no one left to contest her claim to the throne.

Early in 37 BC, the triumvirs renewed their agreement for another five years. Octavia's influence was one of the main reasons. She was trying to avoid conflict between her husband and her brother. But beneath the surface, tensions were steadily increasing. Later that year, Antony left Italy and headed east to launch his campaign against the Parthians. Octavia accompanied him as far as the Greek island of Corfu. Because she was pregnant, he sent her back to Rome. However, this may have been an excuse to get Octavia out of the way so that Antony could be reunited with Cleopatra.

As soon as he arrived in the Syrian city of Antioch, he sent for the Queen. On a personal level, they must have been delighted to be with each other again. According to some historians, they were married at this time. In Egypt, having more than a single spouse was legal. In Rome, it wasn't.

Larger issues were involved as well. Antony needed the money, supplies and ships that she could provide. In turn, Cleopatra demanded land. Antony agreed to give her control of much of his territory, including Cyprus, the Cilician coast (the southern part of modern-day Turkey), Phoenicia (today's Lebanon), and Syria. Cleopatra soon began issuing coins that featured her image on one side and Antony's on the other.

Antony's actions upset many of his fellow Romans. They were outraged that he appeared to have abandoned his lawful wife. They were equally outraged that he gave away Roman lands to a foreigner.

Soon they had even more cause for distress. Not even Cleopatra's support would help Antony in his campaign against the Parthians, which began early in 36 BC. He was defeated and had to retreat later that year. He lost nearly half his army.

One of the few bright spots that year came when Cleopatra bore Antony a third child. The child was a son named Ptolemy Philadelphus.

Back in Rome, Octavia had remained true to Antony in spite of his scandalous behavior. Early in 35 BC, she decided to visit him. She got as far as Athens, one of the leading cities in Greece. There she learned that Antony was not going to meet her. According to Plutarch, Cleopatra played a major role in his decision. She was afraid that Antony might desert her, just as he had seemingly deserted Octavia a few years earlier. It was much more than personal. If Antony returned to Octavia, she would work to resolve his differences with Octavian. If that happened, Cleopatra's protection would be gone. Egypt would be vulnerable to Roman conquest.

So she resorted to exaggerated displays of love, fainting spells and crying. She may have even said that she would die if he left her. In the end, she got her way. Antony eventually sent word to Octavia to return home. He had made his decision. He and Cleopatra were now united, for better or for worse.

Cleopatra was pleased, but the Roman people were furious with the manner in which Antony was treating Octavia. As if that wasn't enough to fuel their anger, Antony staged a Triumph when he returned from a victorious military campaign in Armenia in 34 BC. A Triumph was an elaborate celebration, the highest honor that Rome could offer a victorious military commander. It could only be conferred by the Senate. For Antony to give one to himself, in a foreign city, seemed to be a direct slap to Rome.

Soon afterward, he went even further. He gave important titles to the children he had had with Cleopatra. In a ceremony that became known as the Donations of Alexandria, Antony made Alexander Helios the king of Armenia, Cleopatra Selene became the queen of Cyrenaica and Crete, and Ptolemy Philadelphus was named the king of Syria. Antony also dubbed Caesarion the "King of Kings," and called Cleopatra the "Queen of Kings."

It was an elaborate, very colorful ritual that radiated power and confidence. It was also the beginning of the end for Cleopatra and Antony.

## Hot or Not?

For Your Info

Cleopatra was able to woo some of the richest, most powerful rulers in all of history. Because of that, it is widely assumed that Cleopatra's beauty was breathtaking.

Maybe not.

According to articles published in the British media around the time of a Cleopatra exhibit at London's British Museum in 2001, her beauty has been quite exaggerated over the years. Some of these articles stated she was hook-nosed, plump and had very bad teeth. A typical article maintained that "Cleopatra, the queen of ancient Egypt who seduced Julius Caesar and Mark Antony with her supposedly irresistible beauty, has been revealed as short, frumpish and in need of a good dentist…eleven statues show the queen as plain looking with a streak of sternness, and (she) appears to be plump."[2]

Other authorities argue that she was quite beautiful. Many statues from her time and coins showing her head support that line of thinking. They reveal a royal-looking woman with strong features and wide eyes. The coins show a fine, pointed nose—fit for a queen.

The "plump" accusation might also be challenged. In fact, some historians have said her diet was well-balanced and healthy, consisted mostly of fruit, vegetables, meat and fish.

The curators of the British Museum played it safe, saying that very few portraits of Cleopatra survived, and those that did survive are very inconsistent. The fact is that nobody really knows for sure whether the queen was perfectly lovely or ugly.

However, many Egyptologists have a hard time believing that Caesar would have put up a golden statue of Cleopatra in the Temple of Venus in Rome if she were homely. After all, she was the first living human to share a temple with a Roman god—a tribute to her beauty and heavenly attributes from Caesar himself.

One thing is for sure. She was pretty popular with men like Marc Antony and Julius Caesar, so she had something going for her.

Cleopatra had a real way with people, but she became a victim to a smear campaign orchestrated by Octavian. He printed untrue things about her, convincing Romans that she was immoral and a threat to Rome.

## CHAPTER
# FIVE

# THE END OF A DYNASTY

For several years, Octavian had been building up his strength. In 36 BC, he defeated Lepidus in a battle. That destroyed the already fragile Second Triumvirate and locked him into a power struggle with Antony. Octavian knew he had to proceed cautiously. It spite of everything that Antony had done in the past few years, he still retained some popularity in Rome. And the forces under Antony's command were formidable.

When he learned of the Donations of Alexandria, Octavian showed his genius at propaganda. He began a smear campaign against Antony and Cleopatra. He said that Antony was dressing like an Egyptian rather than a Roman. He accused Antony of falling under the spell of an evil woman. In male-dominated Rome, that was a serious accusation. Octavian said that Antony was going to put Romans under the rule of Egyptians. There was some truth to this assertion. Some of the lands included in the Donations were Roman. Antony had no right, legal or otherwise, to give them to his children.

Octavian compared his sister with Cleopatra. He said that Octavia was a virtuous woman who had been wronged by a faithless husband. On the other hand, Cleopatra was immoral. He cited many examples

*Mark Antony, pictured here, was a great warrior. He was also quite in love with Cleopatra. He eventually divorced his wife Octavia, the sister to Octavian, and married Cleopatra.*

of Antony's and Cleopatra's drunkenness and lavish lifestyle. Not all of them were true.

He even broke into the sacred temple in Rome where Antony had put his will. He claimed that according to the will, Antony wanted to be buried in Alexandria rather than Rome. He also claimed that Antony had made his children with Cleopatra his heirs, not the ones he had with Octavia. These disclosures made many Romans believe that Antony had turned his back on Rome.

Antony fought back. He wanted to convince Romans that he had legitimate complaints against Octavian. But he was hundreds of miles away. It was harder for him to make his case. Finally, probably in 32 BC, he officially divorced Octavia.

By then, both sides believed that war was inevitable. The conflict became official when Octavian publicly declared war in the summer of 32 BC. In a final stroke of propaganda, he declared war only on Cleopatra. Rome had already suffered through several recent civil wars. Octavian hoped that singling out Cleopatra would make the approaching battles seem like a war against a threatening foreigner and attract more people to his side.

It didn't attract several hundred senators who fled to Antony, believing that he would win. The two opposing forces finally came together in the spring of 31 BC at Actium, on the western coast of Greece. They settled into fortified camps a few miles apart.

Under the leadership of a brilliant general named Agrippa, Octavian's naval forces won several skirmishes that cut off the supply lines from Egypt. He blockaded the remaining ships in Antony and Cleopatra's fleet. He also kept the troops under his command from fighting Antony's army, which was larger. Time was on Octavian's side. He and Agrippa settled down to wait.

The waiting ended on September 2. With disease, desertion and hunger steadily cutting into his strength, Antony led his ships out to attack. Octavian's ships slowly gained the upper hand. But the outcome was still in doubt when sixty ships under Cleopatra's direct command, which hadn't been part of the original attack, sailed into the open ocean and escaped. Antony immediately followed her. With their leader gone, the rest of his fleet soon surrendered. A few days later, his troops on land also gave up. The Battle of Actium—which historians regard as one of the most important battles of the ancient world—was a resounding victory for Octavian.

By fleeing the fight, Antony showed the world that he was no longer the man of might he once was. He was seen as a traitor to Rome and a weak man who was being led by his emotions. Ironically, Antony had once dealt harshly with deserters from his own army—yet now he had become a deserter himself, the very thing he so despised. Once on board Cleopatra's ship, it's been reported that he sat alone, refusing to see or speak to her.

When he arrived in Alexandria, Antony sailed along the North African coast, hoping to find safety and support. He didn't. He returned to Alexandria, where he lived alone in a hut on the beach, feeling very depressed.

Meanwhile, Cleopatra prepared for the Roman invasion. As always, she was looking out for herself. She offered money to Octavian in the hope that he would let her children continue ruling in her place. She knew that her enemies were closing in, and she also knew that most of her allies had all switched their loyalties to Octavian.

Octavian kept the money, but he was in a superior position and didn't feel that he had to make any deals. According to some reports, he did offer mercy to Cleopatra if she would either execute Antony or surrender him. Nothing came of the offer.

She had one more hope: to drag her ships across the desert to the Gulf of Suez. Then she could sail into the Red Sea and the Arabian Gulf and establish herself in those regions. But that plan ended when hostile Arabs learned of the plan and destroyed the vessels.

Antony eventually moved back in with Cleopatra so they could enjoy some late-night parties and lots of wine. Several years earlier, they had formed a drinking club to celebrate the pleasure they felt in being with each other and with close friends. Now they changed its name to "The Company of the Inseparable in Death" club.

Octavian's army approached Alexandria in the summer of 30 BC. Antony regained his fighting spirit and led a successful cavalry charge against some of Octavian's men, who were exhausted from their long trek. It was his final triumph. Soon afterward, his ships sailed out to meet Octavian's fleet. Rather than fighting, Antony's sailors saluted the Romans with their oars and abandoned him. His cavalry and his foot soldiers did the same thing. It was all over. Witnesses heard him cry out, blaming Cleopatra for betraying him.

By now, Cleopatra had retreated to the safety of her mausoleum, taking many of her treasures with her. She ordered her servants to tell everyone she was dead. When Antony heard the news of Cleopatra's "death," he was heartbroken. It's been said that he cried out, "Why delay any longer, Antony? Fate has taken away the last and only reason for your clinging to life."[1]

He ordered his servant Eros to kill him so that he could be with Cleopatra, but Eros refused. Instead, Eros stabbed himself with his sword. Antony followed his servant's example and fell on his own sword. But he didn't die immediately. He simply passed out.

When his servants revived him, he begged them to finish him off. Afraid and confused, they ran away. Finally, Cleopatra's secretary found Antony and told him that Cleopatra wanted to see him. He was thrilled to learn that his queen was still alive. He had himself carried to Cleopatra's mausoleum.

She was afraid to open the door, fearing that Octavian's soldiers would rush inside and capture her. So she and her two servants let down ropes from a window and pulled him up to her.

According to Plutarch, "Those who were present say that there was never a more pitiful sight than the spectacle of Antony, covered with blood, struggling in his death agonies and stretching out his hands towards Cleopatra as he swung helplessly in the air."[2]

Cleopatra's servants laid Antony across the bed. He told her not to pity him but to remember their past happiness. Then he died.

After Antony's death, Octavian had Cleopatra brought to him. He explained to her that he had no interest in any relationship, negotiation, or reconciliation. He had no use for her. In fact, he told her that he would take her to Rome and display her in chains before thousands of jeering Romans during a triumphal parade.

One can only imagine that Cleopatra's thoughts drifted back to her sister, Arsinoe, who had been humiliated in the same manner. Cleopatra was far too proud to be remembered this way. She carefully plotted to kill herself. According to legend, she ended her life by allowing herself to be bitten by a poisonous snake. The Egyptian

*This drawing depicts the scene of Cleopatra's death. Cunning as usual, Cleopatra is believed to have planned her death down to the last detail. She enjoyed a great feast; bathed; and put on her elaborate queen costume before pressing a poisonous snake to her body and killing herself.*

religion believed that death by a snakebite guaranteed immortality, which might have been why she chose to die that way.

Cleopatra's death marked the end of an era, as she was Egypt's final pharaoh. Within a year, Octavian made her country into a province of Rome.

Her son Caesarion soon followed her in death. As the son of Julius Caesar, he represented a threat to Octavian, who ordered him to be strangled. Octavian was more merciful with Cleopatra's three children with Antony. He sent them back to Rome, where Octavia raised them.

While many bad things have been said and written about Cleopatra, the actual truth about her will never be completely known. Even today, she remains a mystery.

Many people have asked the question, "Just what kind of woman was Cleopatra?" For answers, we have to rely on the men of her day to tell us who she was and why she did so many outrageous, yet calculated, things throughout her life. We'll never know the inner workings of her brilliant mind, but we can assume that she was loyal to her calling as the queen of Egypt. She gave up a great deal—her very life for the cause.

Cleopatra may have been one of several women who bore that name. But she was definitely one of a kind.

# What Killed the Queen?

## FYI
### For Your Info

After Mark Antony died, Cleopatra was devastated. She no longer had the will to carry on. She had lost two great loves, and she knew Octavian would deal harshly with her. Her future looked bleak.

Rather than face humiliation, she wanted to kill herself. Octavian knew she was determined to die. He did not want her to commit suicide. Instead, he wanted her to live so he could humiliate her. His guards kept a close watch on Cleopatra, making sure she didn't try to take her life.

Their watch wasn't close enough. After visiting Antony's tomb, she returned to her mausoleum, took a bath and ordered a feast. While the meal was being prepared, a man arrived with a basket of figs. According to legend, the figs concealed an asp (an Egyptian cobra). Suspecting nothing, the guards let him in.

After she had eaten, Cleopatra wrote a letter, sealed it, and sent it to Octavian. He opened it and found Cleopatra's plea to allow her to be buried in Antony's tomb. Worried that she'd already killed herself, Octavian sent word to his guards.

The word came too late.

The guards burst into Cleopatra's chamber. They found Cleopatra lying dead on her golden bed, in full royal Egyptian costume. One maid was dying. The other was already dead.

No one knows for sure how Cleopatra died, although the snakebite theory seems to be the most accepted. Some accounts say that two pricks were found on Cleopatra's arm, looking much like the marks that a snake's fangs would have made. Plutarch, who saw the medical record, concluded, "What really took place is known to no one, since it was also said that she carried poison in a hollow comb…yet there was not so much as a spot found, or any symptom of poison upon her body, nor was the asp seen within the monument."[3]

Plutarch believed that Cleopatra was too smart to rely on a snake smuggler in order to carry out her death. Instead, he suggested that maybe she cooked up a little poison of her own. Only Cleopatra holds the truth.

## Chronology

| | |
|---|---|
| **69 BC** | Born in Alexandria, Egypt, the daughter of Pharaoh Ptolemy XII |
| **51** | Becomes queen of Egypt, co-ruling with her younger brother Ptolemy XIII, who is 10 |
| **48** | Forced to leave her throne and seek protection; meets Julius Caesar and begins a love affair with him |
| **47** | Is made co-ruler of Egypt with her brother, Ptolemy XIV; goes on Nile River cruise with Caesar; gives birth to Caesarion, her son |
| **46** | Joins Caesar in Rome |
| **44** | Returns to Egypt after Caesar is assassinated |
| **41** | Meets Mark Antony in the city of Tarsus and begins a relationship |
| **40** | Gives birth to Antony's twins, Alexander Helios and Cleopatra Selene |
| **37** | Marries Antony |
| **36** | Gives birth to another son, Ptolemy Philadelphus |
| **34** | Is named "The Queen of Kings" by Antony at the Donation of Alexandria; her children are also given titles |
| **32** | Octavian declares war on her |
| **31** | Is defeated by Octavian's forces at the Battle of Actium |
| **30** | Kills herself following Antony's suicide; is laid to rest with Antony |

## Timeline in History

| | |
|---|---|
| **753 BC** | According to legend, Romulus and Remus found the city of Rome. |
| **510** | The last Roman king is driven from the city and the Roman Republic is founded. |
| **106** | Pompey the Great is born. |
| **100** | Julius Caesar is born in Rome. |
| **80** | Cleopatra's father, Ptolemy XII, becomes pharaoh of Egypt after the former ruler is killed by the resentful people of Alexandria. |
| **78** | Caesar begins his political career. |
| **63** | Octavian is born. |
| **61** | Cleopatra's little brother, Ptolemy XIII, who will eventually rule with her, is born; Caesar is made governor of Farther Spain. |
| **60** | Pompey the Great joins Julius Caesar and Crassus in the First Triumvirate. |
| **59** | Cleopatra's brother Ptolemy XIV, who eventually shares the crown with her, is born; Caesar is elected consul. |
| **58** | The Romans take over Cyprus, which had been part of the Ptolemies' empire for more than 200 years; Ptolemy XII is overthrown by the people of Alexandria, making Cleopatra's two older sisters Cleopatra VI and Berenice co-rulers. |
| **55** | Ptolemy XII regains his throne. |
| **53** | Crassus is killed during a battle with the Parthians. |
| **48** | Caesar defeats Pompey at the Battle of Pharsalus; Pompey flees to Alexandria where Ptolemy XIII's advisers kill him. |
| **47** | Ptolemy XIII drowns in the Nile and Caesar declares Cleopatra and her brother, Ptolemy XIV, co-rulers of Egypt. |
| **44** | Caesar is assassinated. |
| **43** | Mark Antony, Octavian and Lepidus form the Second Triumvirate. |
| **42** | Antony and Octavian defeat Brutus and Cassius at the Battle of Philippi. |
| **41** | Cleopatra's sister, Arsinoe, is murdered. |
| **40** | Mark Antony marries Octavia, who is Octavian's sister. |
| **36** | Antony suffers defeat in his campaign in Parthia; Octavian defeats Lepidus and expels him from the Second Triumvirate. |
| **30** | Octavian takes over Alexandria; Caesarion is strangled to death. |
| **27** | Octavian changes his name to Augustus Caesar. |
| **11** | Octavia dies. |
| **AD 14** | Augustus Caesar dies. |

# Chapter Notes

**CHAPTER ONE**

1. Hughes-Hallett, Lucy. *Cleopatra: Histories, Dreams and Distortions* (New York: HarperCollins, 1990).
http://www.geocities.com/Athens/Thebes/3013/books.html

2. Adel Murad, "Cleopatra's Mystery Lives On."
http://www.touregypt.net/magazine/mag04012001/mag6.htm

**CHAPTER TWO**

1. Andrew Meadows, "Sins of the Fathers," *Cleopatra of Egypt*, edited by Susan Walker and Peter Higgs (Princeton, NJ: Princeton University Press, 2001), p. 23.

2. Ernle Bradford, *Cleopatra,* (New York: Harcourt Brace Jovanovich Inc., 1972), pp. 13-14.

3. "Conspiracy and Death."
http://ancienthistory.about.com/gi/dynamic/offsite.htm?site=http://www.geocities.com/Athens/Academy/9040/caesar.html

4. "Great Caesar: A biography of Gaius Julius Caesar by Plantagenet Somerset Fry." http://ancienthistory.about.com/gi/dynamic/offsite.htm?site=http://www.geocities.com/Athens/Academy/9040/caesar.html

**CHAPTER THREE**

1. Ernle Bradford, *Cleopatra,* (New York, Harcourt Brace Jovanovich Inc., 1972), p. 63.

2. Ibid., p. 81.

**CHAPTER FOUR**

1. "Cleopatra Daughter of the Pharaoh."
www.royalty.nu/Africa/Egypt/Cleopatra.html

2. Adel Murad, "Cleopatra's Mystery Lives On."
http://www.touregypt.net/magazine/mag04012001/mag6.htm

**CHAPTER FIVE**

1. Ernle Bradford, *Cleopatra* (New York: Harcourt Brace Jovanovich Inc., 1972), p. 257.

2. Guida M. Jackson, *Women Who Ruled* (Santa Barbara, California, ABC-CLIO, Inc., 1990), p.53.

3. Barbara Holland, "Cleopatra: What Kind of Woman Was She, Anyway?"
http://www.dushkin.com/olc/genarticle.mhtml?article=18663

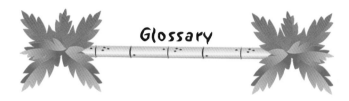

## Glossary

| | |
|---|---|
| **Aphrodite** | (a fro DIE tee)—the Greek goddess of love, corresponding to Venus of the Romans. |
| **barge** | (BARJ)— a pleasure boat, elegantly furnished and decorated. |
| **consul** | (KAHN sul)—the title of a superior Roman leader, similar to today's president. |
| **diplomatic** | (dip low MAT ick)— relating to or characteristic of diplomacy, the art or practice of conducting international relations, as in negotiating alliances, treaties, and agreements. |
| **dowry** | (DOW ree)— money or property brought by a bride to her husband at the time of their marriage. |
| **dynasty** | (DIE nuh stee)—a period when the rulers are all from the same bloodline or family. |
| **Egyptologists** | (ee jip TALL oh jists)—historians who study ancient Egypt. |
| **eunuch** | (YOU nuck)—castrated males; often used in ancient times in high governmental positions because their inability to produce heirs made them no threat to those in power. |
| **exile** | (ECK sile)—forced removal from one's native country. |
| **lyre** | (LIE uhr)—stringed musical instrument like a small harp; often used by the ancients to accompany poetry. |
| **mausoleum** | (mah suh LEE um)—large building built to hold a tomb and treasures belonging to the deceased. |
| **pharaoh** | (FAIR oh)—a king in ancient Egypt. |
| **province** | (PRAH vince)—various lands outside Italy conquered by the Romans and ruled by them as self-contained units. |
| **stature** | (STA chure)—the natural height of a person or animal; relative status of a person. |
| **talents** | (TAL unts)—units of weight and money used in ancient Greece, Rome and the Middle East. |
| **triumvirate** | (try UM vir uht)—a group of three men who controlled the government of the Roman Empire. |
| **Victoria Cross** | (vic TORE ee uh CROSS)—the highest military decoration for heroism awarded to members of the British armed forces. |

## For Further Reading

**For Young Adults**

Deady, Kathleen W. *Ancient Egypt*. Mankato, Minnesota: Capstone Press, 2004.

Hoobler, Dorothy and Tom Hoobler. *Cleopatra (World Leaders Past & Present)*. Philadelphia: Chelsea House Publishers, 1986.

Morgan, Julian. *Cleopatra: Ruling in the Shadow of Rome*. New York: The Rosen Publishing Group, 2003.

Nardo, Don. *The Importance of Cleopatra*. San Diego, California: Lucent Books, 1994.

Streissguth, Tom. *Queen Cleopatra*. Minneapolis, Minnesota: Lerner Publications Company, 2000.

**Works Consulted**

Asimov, Isaac. *The Egyptians*. Boston: Houghton Mifflin Company, 1967.

Bradford, Ernle. *Cleopatra*. New York: Harcourt Brace Jovanovich Inc., 1972.

Casson, Lionel and Editors of TIME-LIFE Books. *Ancient Egypt*. New York: Time-Life Books, 1965.

Fagan, Brian. *Egypt of the Pharaohs*. Washington, D.C.: National Geographic Books, 2001.

Isenberg, Irwin and Richard M. Haywood. *Caesar*. New York: A Horizon Caravel Book, American Heritage Publishing Co., 1964.

Jackson, Guida M. *Women Who Ruled*. Santa Barbara, California, ABC-CLIO, Inc., 1990.

Shaw, Ian. *The Oxford History of Ancient Egypt*. New York: Oxford University Press, 2000.

Walker, Susan and Peter Higgs (editors). *Cleopatra of Egypt*. Princeton, NJ: Princeton University Press, 2001.

## For Further Reading

**On the Internet**

Cleopatra Daughter of the Pharaoh
    http://www.royalty.nu/Africa/Egypt/Cleopatra.html
Queens of Egypt, Part III Cleopatra
    http://www.touregypt.net/magazine/mag04012001/magf4.htm
Gnaeus Pompey Magnus
    http://users2.ev1.net/~legionary/mainevent/coins/GnaeusPompeyMagnus.html
Historical Timeline Ancient Egypt
    http://www.freemaninstitute.com/Gallery/etime.htm
Cleopatra
    http://www.dvdmoviecentral.com/ReviewsText/cleopatra.htm
Trivia for Cleopatra
    http://www.imdb.com/title/tt0056937/trivia
Elizabeth Taylor at Reel Classics
    http://www.reelclassics.com/Actresses/Liz_Taylor/liz5.htm
Cleopatra VII: Ptolemaic Dynasty
    http://interoz.com/egypt/cleopatr.htm
Julius Caesar
    http://www.incwell.com/Biographies/Caesar.html
Cleopatra's Mystery Lives On
    http://www.touregypt.net/magazine/mag04012001/mag6.htm
Queens of Egypt, Part III: Cleopatra http://www.touregypt.net/magazine/mag04012001/
    magf4.htm
Holland, Barbara. "Cleopatra: What Kind of Woman Was She, Anyway?"
    http://www.dushkin.com/olc/genarticle.mhtml?article=18663
Ptolemaic Dynasty – Ptolemy I - XV
    http://www.crystalinks.com/ptolemaic.html
Cleopatra
    http://www.channel4.com/history/microsites/H/history/rome/cleopatra.html

# Index